Devil's Cheat Sheet

Denay, Binary, Octal, and Hexadecimal

Lewis Mortimer

V 1.0

Devil's Cheat Sheet – Denary, Binary, Octal, and Hexadecimal

ISBN-10: 1544082657

ISBN-13: 978-1544082653

Editor: *Lewis Mortimer*

Illustrator: *Misty Mortimer*

Table of Contents

Denary

- Denary is the standard number system used throughout the world
- It is also known as the "decimal system" or as a "base ten system"
- It uses ten digits:
  - 0,1,2,3,4,5,6,7,8,9
- When using multiple number systems together, it is good practise to use 9457_{10} to show that the number is in denary.

Counting in Denary

- To count above 9 in denary, another column is added, this is known as the tens column, then the hundreds column and then the thousands column

Thousands	Hundreds	Tens	Units
			7
		5	
	4		
9			

- In denary, each digit from right to left is multiplied by ten to the corresponding power, for example:
  - $7*1(10^0) + 5*10(10^1) + 4*100(10^2) + 9*1000(10^3) =$
  - $7 + 50 + 400 + 9000 = 9457$

Advantages of the Denary System

- Is easily divisible by 2 and 5 and therefore by all numbers that aren't prime
- Humans typically have 10 fingers which can aid in adding numbers
- Is taught through the world and is a "universal language"

Disadvantages of the Denary System

- Must be converted into a range of other number systems in order to be compatible with computers:
  - Binary
  - Octal
  - Hexadecimal
- Other number systems, such as hexadecimal, can be divided by a greater selection of numbers as well as primes
- The Gregorian calendar and standard clocks are not divisible using denary

Binary

- Binary is a number system that only uses two numbers: 0 and 1.
- Information processed by computers is in the form of a sequence of ones and zeroes.
- This binary system is known as a "base two system" as there are only two digits to select from.
- When using this system, data is converted using the power of 2.
- A binary digit is called a "bit", short for "binary digit".
- When pronouncing a binary number out loud, each digit should be pronounced individually, for example:
    - 1010 should be pronounced as one zero one zero and not one thousand and ten.
- To show that a number is a binary number, it should be followed with a 1010_2.

Denary	8	7	6	5	4	3	2	1
Binary	1000	111	110	101	100	11	10	1
Binary Place Values	128 Most Significant	64	32	16	8	4	2	1 Least Significant

- By using 8 binary place values, a user can create any number from 0 to 255. For example:
    - 128+32+16+4+2+1=183
- In subnetting and networking this is especially prominent as IPv4 addresses are comprised of 4 octets (a group of 8 bits).
    - A typical IPv4 address may look like this:
        - 192.168.0.1
    - Translated into a binary number, it would look like this:
        - 11000000.10101000.00000000.00000001

- Computers can only understand numbers, so an ASCII code (American Standard Code for Information Interchange) is used as a numerical representation of characters such as "A" or "!".

- The word "Binary" has these numerical decimal values for each letter the word contains:
  - "B" – 66   "i" – 105   "n" – 110   "a" – 97   "r" – 114   "y" – 121
- These decimal values can be translated into binary:
  - "66" – 0100 0010   "105" – 0110 1001   "110" – 0110 1110   "97" – 0111 0010   "121" – 0111 1001
- 128   64   32   16   8   4   2   1
- B = 66   64+2=66
- All numbers used are represented by a 1, all other numbers not used remain at 0. Working from left to right we can determine the answer is:
  - 01000010

Counting in Binary

Decimal	2^3	2^2	2^1	Binary 2^0
	8	4	2	1
0 =	0	0	0	0
1 =	0	0	0	1
2 =	0	0	1	0
3 =	0	0	1	1
4 =	0	1	0	0
5 =	0	1	0	1
6 =	0	1	1	0
7 =	0	1	1	1
8 =	1	0	0	0

Advantages of the Binary System
- Very simple as it works on a true/false "Boolean" logic, ie:
  - Is there a presence or absence of an electrical current?
- Works well with computers physically as they operate using switches and logic gates
- Provides a very low possibility of error; is the switch on or off?
- Requires the fewest number of numerals

Disadvantages of the Binary System
- Only present in certain situations such as computing or networking
- Often requires conversion into decimal systems
- Other systems can express numbers in shorter strings ie:
  - (Decimal) 66
  - (Binary) 01000010
- Binary representations are generally too long for humans to remember

Octal

- Octal is a numbering system that uses a base of 8 as opposed to 10 for denary or 2 for binary.
- The single-digit numbers used consist of:
  - 0,1,2,3,4,5,6,7
- In octal, a binary number is divided into groups of 3 bits that offer a value from "000" (0) to "111" (7)
- The octal number system provides a convenient method of converting large binary numbers into smaller numbers. For instance
  - 8 bits equal a byte
  - 56 bits can be translated into 7 bytes
- To show that a number is an octal number, it should be followed with a 376_8

Counting in Octal

- To count above 7 in octal, another column is added, similar to hexadecimal or denary:
  - 0,1,2,3,4,5,6,7   10,11,12,13,14,15,16,17   20
  - 10 is not to be confused with ten, the number is simply 1+0

8^8	8^7	8^6	8^5	8^4	8^3	8^2	8^1	8^0
16,000,000	2,000,000	262,000	32,000	4,000	512	64	8	1

Denary	3-bit Binary	Octal
0	000	0
1	001	1
2	010	2
3	011	3
4	100	4
5	101	5
6	110	6
7	111	7
8	001 000	10 (1+0)
9	001 001	11 (1+1)
10	001 010	12 (1+2)

- As shown above, the binary digits are split into groups of three in octal. A number such as 1101100111 should be split like this:
  - 1 101 100 111
  - As we can see, one of the groups has a digit by itself; to rectify this we fill the group with 0s
    - 001 101 100 111

Advantages of the Octal System

- Octal can very concisely represent bit patterns
- Octal can greatly reduce the exact value of large chunks of data
- Can be used on numeric-only displays whereas hexadecimal cannot

Disadvantages of the Octal System

- Octal is outdated and Hexadecimal is the preferred choice as most systems use eight-bit bytes
- Octal is not typically used outside of computing and has been mostly replaced by larger base number systems

Hexadecimal

- Hexadecimal is a numbering system that uses a base of 16
- The single-digits used consist of:
  - 0,1,2,3,4,5,6,7,8,9,A,B,C,D,E,F
  - These are called hex digits and reflect a 4-bit binary sequence called a "nibble"
- Hexadecimal is a convenient way of expressing binary numbers in computing as a byte contains 8 binary bits
- A byte contains 2 nibbles or 2 4-bit binary sequences
- An example of a hexadecimal and it's binary equivalent could be:

Hexadecimal	A2E
Denary digit values	A=10 2=2 E=14
Binary	1010 0010 1110

- To show that a number is a hexadecimal number, it should be followed with a $A2E_{16}$

Counting in Hexadecimal

- To count above 15 in octal, another column is added, similar to octal or denary:
    - 0,1,2,3,4,5,6,7,8,9   A,B,C,D,E,F   10,
    - 10 is not to be confused with ten, the number is simply 1+0

Denary	Hexadecimal	Binary
0	0	0
1	1	1
2	2	10
3	3	11
4	4	100
5	5	101
6	6	110
7	7	111
8	8	1000
9	9	1001
10	A	1010
11	B	1011
12	C	1100
13	D	1101
14	E	1110
15	F	1111
16	10	10000
17	11	10001
18	12	10010
19	13	10011
20	14	10100

Advantages of the Hexadecimal System

- Hexadecimal can be used to simplify how binary is represented:
  - 1010111101101001 = AF69
- A base of 2 can be converted easily into a base of 16:
  - $16 = 2_4$
- Base 16 corresponds well with memory addressing in computers:
  - 1 byte is equal to two hexadecimal digits
- Hexadecimal can be used to represent colours in image editing programs using the format #RRGGBB (r = red, g = green, and b = blue)
  - In binary 1111 1111 is FF and holds a possible 256 possible combinations for that colour
  - 256 * 256 * 256 equals 16,777,216 possible colour combinations

Disadvantages of the Hexadecimal System

- Requires the user to know the binary system and be able to convert it into hexadecimal
- Mathematical equations using "A-F" have no way of being able to distinguish between the numbers in hexadecimal and the variables:
  - $A + 1 = x$ $B + 2 = y$
- Cannot be used on numeric-only displays as hexadecimal contains letters

Conversion Methods

Converting Binary to Denary and Denary to Binary

- To convert a binary number to a denary number, it's a good idea to write out the binary place values. This is to make it easier to add the numbers together.
- Select the number to convert, in this case we will use "47"
- Looking at the place holders, and working from left to right, determine which is the highest number that can fit into "47"
- Enter a "1" into the binary placeholder and subtract the binary place value from "47" (47 – 32 = 15)
- Continue working from left to right and fill in all placeholders that make up the number "47"
  - (15 – 8 = 7)
  - (7 – 4 = 3)
  - (3 – 2 = 1)
  - (1 – 1 = 0)
- All placeholders that were not used should be filled with a "0"
- The table below shows the correct answer when converting the denary number to binary.
- To confirm this, we can work backwards and convert the binary back into denary as shown in the third row of the below chart.

128	64	32	16	8	4	2	1	Binary Placeholder
0	0	1	0	1	1	1	1	Binary = 00101111
0+	0+	32+	0+	8+	4+	2+	1	Denary = 47

Converting Binary to Octal and Octal to Binary

- To convert a binary number to an octal number, the binary must be separated into 3-bit binary groups starting from the right and working to the left
- These groups can then be converted into denary, for example:
  - $101_2 = 4+1=5_8$
- For multiple groups, the same technique is used:
  - 101_2 $110_2 = 4+1=5_8$ and $4+2=6_8$
  - The denary, binary and octal conversions are shown below

Binary	101110
Octal	101 110 = 4+1=5 and 4+2=6 5 6$_8$

- To convert an octal number to a binary number, each digit in the octal number must be separated and converted to binary using 3-bit binary groups
- "5 6$_8$" turns into 5 and 6 which turns into 101 and 110
- Binary does not use bit groups and so 101 and 110 come together to make 101110

Converting Binary to Hexadecimal and Hexadecimal to Binary

- Split the binary number into 4-bit binary groups, also known as "nibbles":
  - 10101111 = 1010 1111
- Calculate the total value of each nibble
  - 1010 = 10 1111 = 15
- By looking at the table below, we know that the hexadecimal equivalents of 10 and 15 are A and F
- Therefore, 10101111 = AF

Denary	Hexadecimal	Binary
0	0	0
1	1	1
2	2	10
3	3	11
4	4	100
5	5	101
6	6	110
7	7	111
8	8	1000
9	9	1001
10	A	1010
11	B	1011
12	C	1100
13	D	1101
14	E	1110
15	F	1111
16	10	10000
17	11	10001
18	12	10010
19	13	10011
20	14	10100

- Working backwards from the hexadecimal number "AF" we need to split the values of A and F into 4-bit binary groups, also known as "nibbles":
  - A = 1010   F = 1111
    - It can be helpful for beginners to convert the hexadecimal number to denary before converting to binary
      - A = 10_{10} = 1010_2 F = 15_{10} = 1111_2
- Once the hexadecimal number has been converted into 4-bit binary groups, remove the spacing between each group:
  - 1010 1111 = 10101111
- We can conclude this is the correct answer by referring back to the previous exercise

Converting Denary to Octal and Octal to Denary

- To convert denary numbers into octal we must divide the denary number by 8
- The answers are then divided by 8 until there is a final result of 0
- The remainders become the next most significant digit in the octal result

Denary	Division	Answer	Remainders	Octal
3478	/8	434	6	6
434	/8	54	2	26
54	/8	6	6	626
6	/8	0	6	6626
0	Complete			

   - As we can see, the answer is 6626
- To convert octal to denary start by adding 0 to the most significant octal digit
   - (0 + 3 = 3)
- Multiply the result by 8
   - (3 * 8 = 24)
- Take the denary result and add the next most significant octal digit
   - (24 + 4 = 28)
- Multiply the result by 8
   - (28 * 8 = 224)
- Continue adding the octal digits and multiplying by 8 until there is only one octal digit remaining
- Once there is only one octal digit remaining, add it to the denary result and stop, you are finished

Octal	Addition	Result	Multiply	Denary Result
345	0 + 3	3	*8	24
45	24 + 4	28	*8	224
5	224 + 5	229	Complete	229

Converting Denary to Hexadecimal and Hexadecimal to Denary

- To convert a denary number to a hexadecimal number, we must divide the number by 16:
  - 5692 /16 = 355 with a remainder of 12 = C
    - The table below must be used to obtain the hexadecimal digit if the remainder is greater than decimal 9
  - Continue dividing all answers by 16 until no longer possible
    - 255 / 16 = 22 with a remainder of 3
    - 22 / 16 = 1 with a remainder of 6
    - 1 / 16 = 0 with a remainder of 1
  - Once there is only one digit remaining, you are finished

Decimal	Division	Answer	Remainder	Hexadecimal
5692	/16	355	12 = C	C
355	/16	22	3	3C
22	/16	1	6	63C
1	/16	0	1	163C

Denary	Hexadecimal
6	6
7	7
8	8
9	9
10	A
11	B
12	C
13	D
14	E
15	F

- To convert a hexadecimal number to a denary number, we must multiply each digit by an increasing power of 16:
    - $163C = (1 * 16^3 (4096)) + (6 * 16^2 (1536)) + (3 * 16^1 (48)) + (C/12 * 1 (12))$
    - $4096 + 1536 + 48 + 12 = 5692$

Converting Octal to Hexadecimal and Hexadecimal to Octal

- When converting octal to hexadecimal it is easier to convert the octal number into binary first and then into hexadecimal:
  - Octal 4 3 6 = Binary 100 011 110 = 100011110
- Once the binary equivalent is found, split the result into 4-digit binary groups starting from right to left:
  - 100011110 = 0001 0001 1110
    - 0s can be added to fill a group to 4 digits
  - These binary groups can then be converted into hexadecimal
    - 0001 = 1   0001 = 1   1110 = E

Hexadecimal	Binary
0	0
1	1
2	10
3	11
4	100
5	101
6	110
7	111
8	1000
9	1001
A	1010
B	1011
C	1100
D	1101
E	1110
F	1111

- By combining the result from each binary group conversion, we can see that the answer is "11E"

- To convert hexadecimal to octal, it is easier to convert the hexadecimal number into binary first and then into octal:
  - Hexadecimal 1 1 E = Binary 0001 0001 1110 = 100011110
- Once the binary equivalent is found, split the result into 3-digit binary groups starting from right to left:
  - 100011110 = 100 011 110
    - 0s can be added to fill a group to 3 digits
  - These binary groups can then be converted into octal
    - 100 = 4   011 = 3   110 = 6

Octal	Binary
0	0
1	1
2	10
3	11
4	100
5	101
6	110
7	111

- By combining the result from each binary group we can see that the answer is "436"

Denary – Binary – Octal – Hexadecimal

Conversion Chart

Denary	Binary	Octal	Hexadecimal
0	0	000	0
1	1	001	1
2	10	002	2
3	11	003	3
4	100	004	4
5	101	005	5
6	110	006	6
7	111	007	7
8	1000	010	8
9	1001	011	9
10	1010	012	A
11	1011	013	B
12	1100	014	C
13	1101	015	D
14	1110	016	E
15	1111	017	F
16	10000	020	10
17	10001	021	11
18	10010	022	12
19	10011	023	13
20	10100	024	14